Angel Rain

Angel Rain

Art Beck
poems 1977–2020

SHANTI ARTS PUBLISHING
BRUNSWICK, MAINE

Angel Rain

Published by Shanti Arts Publishing
Designed by Shanti Arts Designs

Cover image is a funerary statue of a siren. In Greek mythology, sirens were creatures who lured mariners with irresistable song, leading them to shipwreck on rocky coasts. But in another guise, they were sacred to Persephone and acted as *psychopomps*, guides to the dead and melodic consolers as they entered the paths of the afterlife. This marble figure flanked the *stele* of an Athenian warrior who fell in combat around 395 BCE. It is housed in the National Archeological Museum, Athens, Greece. Photograph is attributed to "Marsyas" on Wikimedia Commons (CC BY-SA 3.0).

Shanti Arts LLC
193 Hillside Road
Brunswick, Maine 04011
shantiarts.com

Printed in the United States of America

ISBN: 978-1-951651-76-3 (softcover)

Library of Congress Control Number: 2022941823

Contents

Angelic Pleasures

Dream Politics

Ancestors

Homage to Ithaca

Departures

Acknowledgments

Versions of many of these poems appeared in various small and university press journals and anthologies over several decades.

These include the print magazines:
Americarna, Artful Dodge, Caprice, Free Lunch, Invisible City, One Trick Pony, OR, Painted Bride Quarterly, Passager, Pinchpenny, Rattle, Ribot, Sequoia, Sho, The Temple, Thorny Locust, Tule Review, Swamproot, Vagabond, as well as the blogsites, Big Bridge, Yu News, and *Medusa's Kitchen*

The anthologies:
California Poetry from the Gold Rush to the Present (Heyday Books); *New Works* (Duckdown Press); and *Painted Bride Quarterly's 25 Year Retrospective, The Vagabond Anthology,* and *Once More With Feeling* (Vagabond Press)

The chapbooks:
The Discovery of Music (Vagabond, 1977); *Summer with All Its Clothes Off* (Gravida, 2005); and *The Insistent Island* (Magra Books, 2019)

Foreword

by Paul Vangelisti

I've been publishing Art Beck's poetry and translations for
some forty-five years, and it seems almost redundant to say
that *Angel Rain* is long-overdue.

With Beck's poetry, a dynamic immediately emerges:
a precision derived from a language that, in Dr. Johnson's
terms, "reeks of the human." That is, a relentless impulse
for clarity embodied in a language teeming with the
physical world and its experience. One has only to look
at the first poems in the collection, for instance, "The
Insistent Fragrance of the Sun," to find the dynamic at
work:

> The most terrifying aspect of aging
> is that the less desirable I become,
> the more intensely I desire.
> Is it any wonder that love
> rhymes so naturally with sorrow?

One should note that clarity doesn't preclude a poem's
musicality, as in the exquisitely painful verses of the second
part of the book, "Dream Politics." Illuminations follow
one upon the other, reinforcing, in an often unsettling way,
the sense of the poem's disregard for sentimentality: its
aloofness, perhaps even cruelty, in regard to individual
sentiment (from "In Ovid the Flaying"):

> What was Marsyas thinking? Certainly, not
> what seething, insulted divinity had in mind.
>
> Was it any comfort his meadow-blood clarified
> and wept as it seeped beneath the grass—then

welled and flowed anew as it became
the purest spring in Phrygia?

Notwithstanding the delight in quoting Beck's verses,
one hesitates to schematize this work, offering a description
of words, insisting in their cogent energy, to aspire beyond
paraphrase, beyond common utility. Utility, however, isn't
lost but, as the conclusion to "Croatian Wedding" testifies, is
arrestingly transformed. Where the poet appears a spectator
to an ethnic celebration, he finds himself unexpectedly
transported as a member of a larger, all too human community:

Christ, whose first miracle
was to make water into wine for man's happiness,
has been ritually betrayed, crucified, and buried again.
But the smiling glow in his gut (and the tiny
bride, holding her swollen belly out like a tabernacle)
remind the priest in a sudden Eucharistic revelation
that it wasn't proud Peter, loyal John, or the perfect
Blessed Virgin—but sweet, slutty Magdalene,
who was first to be entrusted
with the news of the resurrection.
Without love, we're nothing.

In the fourth section, "Homage to Ithaca," we have
some of Beck's most recent, and I must say, accomplished
and challenging work. It's the fruit of his many years as
a translator who remains as uncompromising with his
versions of Latin and German as with his own poetry. Beck
is fond of reminding us that translating poetry is like writing
it, only harder. In his reworkings of episodes from Homer's
Odyssey, the poet displays a remarkable mastery of subject.
His Penelope, Telemachus, Circe, Cyclops, Kalypso, Nausicaa,
even the faithful dog Argus, come to life with a compelling

familiarity. It's the fact of these impossible lives, so strange and so strangely familiar, that makes the poems resonate. In "Kalypso," Mercury brings greetings from cousin Circe, as well as news that Odysseus is on his way. The besieged traveler, notes the enchantress, is at least worth a casual or not-so-casual dalliance. Kalypso then asks the messenger god the intriguing question:

> "What is it Circe sees in mortals, Hermes?"
> The messenger god coughed, then mimicked
> Circe's lazy, curious voice: "Like the rest of them,
> he has that fascinating fragrance of death.
> But he's smarter than most. He sees
> it clearly, and he doesn't whine."

Beck's version of Odysseus's long exile with Kalypso is the most comprehensive in "Homage to Ithaca," and one of the finest and most moving pieces in the sequence, if not the entire book. It underscores the central subject of Beck's variations on Odysseus's fate, the hero's insistence on being human, i.e. mortal, refusing Kalypso's gift of quasi-immortality. In its simple, overwhelming conclusion, the goddess doesn't look away but is surely taken with Odysseus's mortality, if ever so graciously:

> The morning he finally, sheepishly
> asked if he might be allowed to go
> home to die with his old wife—I thought—
> "I've had the best of him. The rest
> is nothing but loss. Better all at once
> than watching this little by little."

> So we built a nice little boat and I tied
> my scarf around his neck. I felt quite

magnanimous, quite divine. It wasn't until
I saw how he skipped like a boy into the waves
and looked back laughing that I wondered:
Had I really been such a burden?

What we have in this collection of poetry, spanning some
forty-five years, is a tireless insistence on precision and
directness, and the attendant conviction that directness
allows for the most enduring music. It's not so much a style
or mode of writing but an implacable vision, what a poet
aspires to in draft after draft of a poem. As life advances,
understanding, one hopes, grows more forgiving and
perhaps serene, though no less demanding.

A few words about the book's title, *Angel Rain*. By the
poet's own admission in a recent email, Angel Rain was
never a working title for the collection, rather a leitmotif
that surfaced as the book was assembled from decades of
work. Also, according to the poet, the title suggests "some
residual fallen-away Catholic entity quietly resting in a more
than incidental number of these poems."

In the book's final section, "Departures," death is a
present subject, as in the second poem, "Broken April,"
concluding with the inescapable:

The rain

is what roots you.
Death only happens once in a lifetime,

but your time revolves around it
like an invisible sun.

The music of Beck's poetry, in its articulate syntax,
is no more evident in its maturity than in "Non fui, fui,

non sum ...," the Epicurean motto popular on Roman tombstones. An elegy for a lost friend, it's also a homage to the poet's translations of Martial and other Roman classics, wherein the marmoreal Latin serves as theme and variation for the poet's grieving:

> Where did our laughter live
>
> until we met, that lifetime ago? Or before
> we were even born, those million, trillion
> years we weren't? There'll be millions,
>
> trillions more when we aren't. But
> Annie, for a little while, just talking
> on this lost silly earth, we were.

The rest may indeed be silence, but all the more urgent for the rigorous music upholding it.

Angelic Pleasures

Flying Dreams

In those suddenly liberating dreams,
we don't levitate—but swim. It's beneath
the surface that we soar. And so
the miracle isn't flight—but breath.

Defeat

The poor man's hope is not
that he'll be spared defeat,
but that, maybe, he'll be able
to negotiate.

The rich, on the other
hand, dream constantly
of total victory. Their
ruin is complete.

Viagra

Because even at the best of times,
the worst can happen.

Because as we grow old,
we grow more timid.

Because young women are frightening.

Because sometimes old guys who finally decide
to cash it all in on the trophy find
they don't have a hook to hang it on.

Because that old insatiable Parisian count
in Casanova—who'd spared no woman
from princess to stable girl—
was disgraceful in his dotage

when he could no longer manage
and tried, again and again, then

shrugged and wiggled his powdered ass
at the "wristband" boys, declared:
"One must make the best of any situation."

The Insistent Fragrance of the Sun

The most terrifying aspect of aging
is that the less desirable I become,
the more intensely I desire.
Is it any wonder that love
rhymes so naturally with sorrow?

Not Quite Casablanca, But . . .

Suddenly our lives
are like 1942 in Yugoslavia.
You, the lovely, widowed partisan,
me, the parachuted British spy.
You bring your forest secrets to my
city flat to be radioed to Churchill,
who's struggling to save
modern civilization. Then we concentrate our
energies on resurrecting the ancient world.

Who's to say how many days are left for us?
The wireless keeps warning me to be ready.
Who's to say we haven't used them all?
The little gods of pleasure
in our things, that played like butterflies
and hummingbirds together, are
already contemplating an angelic sulk.
When we leave—I tell you—I think

this neighborhood will be dismantled like a dream.
Hitler's tanks will flatten
the gingerbread houses, machine gunners
will scour the dusty alleys for our traces.
You shudder against my neck and say,
"a sense of loss will be our only souvenir"

but can't suppress an experienced wink.
When we go our separate ways
what's lost but that lovekiller,
time, like an old grandfather Stalin
hypnotized by sun and wine in our buzzing
summer garden while, fingers on each
other's parting lips, we quietly
escape to carry on the liberation.

Catechism

The sexual pleasures of the initiated angels
are many, but chiefly consist of inhabiting
curious sinners like us for a day,
an hour, a moment: heaven
blushes at our innocent touch

Sierra Autumn

How could you begin to talk about just human
cruelty without noticing how tender the air
becomes, making up its mind to attack.
Without noticing the birches and poplars

shrugging off every superfluous memory, the way
a defeated people will bury whatever's left of themselves
—then bury the maps. Put on their oldest, most
ordinary clothes, their most indecipherable smiles.

I keep imagining those cruel kisses spread out on
the boulder between us like coins we can count—then slip, one
by one, into the river. Your undetectable, childish fingers.

Anyone would think the three of us are just peacefully watching
the delicate, dead gold leaves shower around our shoulders,
hypnotized by the futile richness of the end of a season

The Fall from Grace

Something happened to us.
We sense it in our genes.
Whether it was the rebuff
of a secret garden

or an errant spaceship
marooned light years from
home on a hopeless
world—somewhere, somehow, long

ago, we lost something, too painfully
to recall. Something so lovely
our blood can't forget.

Music remembers, wine
remembers, and lovers, like drunken
angels, console their helpless wings.

Croatian Wedding

San Jose, California, 1987

Jesus, this is no place to bring blonde
Protestants. None of your modern nuns with blue
bonnets and stylish stockings here. The two
lurking in the shadows behind the organ,
wrapped up like black widows of Christ and
smelling like paper, have the faces
of winter oaks. The priest must have been born

with that bushy eyed Slavic scowl. And even though
the wedding party's dressed in white, pink and baby
blue and strolls up the aisle to Mendelssohn,
the ceremony still begins with the medieval ritual
of churchly guilt.

"Examine . . . repent . . . confess . . . Lamb
of God who takest away . . .
O Lord I am not worthy . . . Now and at the hour of
our death . . . " Old men from the terrible old
country nod their heads, cross themselves,
and ask the inlaid floor for mercy.
Old women with vicious memories mutter their *mea
culpas*, but know it's not their business to forgive.

Outside the open doors on the sunny lawn, the wedding
lamb relaxes on its spit, crackling tubs of ice
wait patiently for whiskey. The orchestra
makes whispery, testing noises under the ribboned trees.
A baby begins to wail in the corner.
The saucy two year old, three rows up, lifts her skirt
to show the boy behind her something interesting.

And the groom, his eye on the door, but as
serious as Jugoslavia, begins to read an excerpt from
Genesis to the congregation. He winces as if it were his
own rib God was taking. His nineteen year old, American
bride—eight months pregnant and worried she'll
lose her water—is sent to the pulpit next.
She shyly works her way through St. Paul's tongues
and angels, wants to giggle once but hides it
with a cough. Father Janos (he tolerates but

can hardly approve) takes charge again.
He quickly marries them and then the mass
begins. His mind is on sin, grief and wine.
He sermonizes on the feast at Cana: Jesus
rushed by his virgin mother into the wise world before
his time like any tragic draftee. Doing a light
hearted bit of magic to impress the crafty waiters,
but knowing—like a vague toothache—this
was going to lead to nowhere but pain.

The brown robed altar boy brings cruets as
large as table decanters. The priest waves
away the water and watches sternly while his gold
chalice is filled to the top with fortified muscatel.

In honor of the convert bride and the groom's
great, adopted California home, the mass
is said in broken English rather than Latin.
The old priest's consecrating voice is solemn.
"And knowing His hours were numbered, He asked
for his disciples to eat and for to drink with
Him one time more. He began to tear at bread—
Here, eat this, it is my flesh torn from my bones.
And later, after the meal, finishing wine—

This wine is my blood you are drinking."
Father Janos raises the enormous chalice
to his lips with trembling hands. His
adam's apple dispatches the transubstantiated
wine like a machine gun.
All fourteen stations of the cross stare down with bloodshot
owl eyes on the trembling couple. The dissolving
wafers stick to their tongues like glue. Their new rings
squeeze their knuckles. The bride's about to faint,
the groom only knows he needs a drink. July's invaded
the packed church and they're sweating as much as the night
this all started with the fogged car windows shut
tight in the warm Christmas moonlight.

And then the organ sets us free. The nasal Balkan voices
of the powerful nuns lead the congregation in
a processional whose words only the old country
initiates understand. Father Janos, still feeling his triple
slug of fermented divinity, hums along while he walks
with his arms around the captured pair.
His good day's work accomplished he can already

taste cold beer. Christ, whose first miracle
was to make water into wine for man's happiness,
has been ritually betrayed, crucified, and buried again.
But the smiling glow in his gut (and the tiny
bride, holding her swollen belly out like a tabernacle)
remind the priest in a sudden Eucharistic revelation
that it wasn't proud Peter, loyal John, or the perfect
Blessed Virgin—but sweet, slutty Magdelene,
who was first to be entrusted
with the news of the resurrection.
Without love, we're nothing.

Dixieland

In music it's called "theory"—with the implicit
understanding that it's an after the fact
discussion: The way lovers talk about fucking—amazed,
nervous and curious about all the tangled

pleasures they realize they can't help.
But language is more political, more tempted
by the Byzantine ideal, the totalitarian compulsion
for dogma to dominate art. For a musician,

it's like asking Stravinsky to stick to minuets.
Because, trying to fake our sonnet feels like dixieland,
like white college boy jazz—like picking up someone else's

trumpet and clarinet and cadence and meter and long and
short vowels—while our breath slips between the lines,
caught in the echoes of the words I didn't use.

Here It Is, Memorial Day
at Clear Lake Again,

and even after a winter as deep as the hundred year
flood of a winter we had, Annie, the night air
suddenly smells of road dust again, and hay, and even
a trace of skunk. It's only two weeks since serious rain,
but the hill grass is already turning blond at the roots.
Not quite yet, but soon enough and all of a sudden,
I think we might have another summer.
Is it a consolation of age, that sometime around
the middle of flu shivering January, we forget
just how nice July can be? So that each new
summer becomes a fresh revelation of how bright
and quick that fire was, before it sputtered into smoke.

Except when this year's over, I'll be fifty five
and you'll be fifty nine, pumpkin, and while the short
years somersault and rewind themselves like
elegant wristwatches, our bodies keep, their own, straight
ahead, digital time. Fiftieth birthday parties remind me
of Christmas, Annie, a reckless festival of candles
against a patient, relentless night. And I remember your
party—how you began the celebration a good
two weeks early and carried on like the champagne
queen until the month was over. You were an
inspiration to me, hiding behind the curtain
and peeking out the window of what's next.

For myself, when the great day came, I kept as quiet
as a burglar, hoping to steal my holiday
without paying the usual, exorbitant price.
Well, all that's behind us, and so quickly,

too. But I wonder, if like myself, you sometimes
find yourself in the middle of a dream, realizing
you're such and such an age and wondering
how this thing could ever be. What is it
in our dreaming selves that's so startled
the time has passed? What is it that's
beginning to mourn, even in my deepest sleep?
What do I have to let go of to fly?

Artist, Model, Muse

Is it his oils and the glowing kerosene stove
that evoke the ghosts of the old farm animals,
dark and quiet in their straw? Or do they sense

the graying blonde woman posing un-perfumed
for the famous man? Square fingered, middle
aged but muscled, alive, and glorious in her skin.

An angelus of mortal flesh.
The barn, that once welcomed
foals to this world, is pregnant
with her menopausal light. He guards

his eyes, makes just small talk. The brush
no longer guided by his fingers but by the
gentle, relentless curiosity of love. If she
suspected she might never come back.

Cottage

Summer with all its clothes off, meets you at the door
with a mouthful of licorice and roses.
The sinews of peace stretch like cats as you work the cork
from the cold, sweating bottle.
You may as well forget another Monday's
just a week away:
something greener than money's got
hold of you. July's never shy
about anything here, and earth insists
on pulling you back to earth.

Prayer

Virgin Mother of my childhood, take charge
of my huge dog, Bruno. Comfort him
in his confusion, scratch behind his ear
and stroke his nervous back. Tell him not to be foolish

enough to try to attack the three headed, snarling
hound they say keeps watch over the dead.
Remind him he's toothless, shaky and venerable,
and that, lately, he's had more than enough

fights he can't win. Guide him, instead,
to someplace peaceful, a riverside park where people
play ball and barbecue—if that kind of place
exists under the rich green earth he loved so much.

He was a dog made for happiness, and nature
smiled like a beehive when he was born.
Black and brown, son of a tame wolf and half-Labrador,
his markings were perfectly balanced, identical

on each side. A terror to Dobermans and German Shepherds,
raccoon stalker, and clever guardian, angry and controlled—
he grew, from a pup in the palms of my hands, to a hundred
and twenty pounds, and lived for seventeen years.

Strong as a mule, he pulled me up steep hills,
and then—set free—would range right and left,
panting ahead in the trees. Disappearing
and returning, crashing through the underbrush;

he taught me the sweetness of roaming the deep woods
in the company of a large, fierce, animal.
Blessed Mother, take care of him. Despite his uncertain legs,
he came to you in good spirits with proper respect, and

with his brave tail wagging as he licked the hand
of the pretty, curly headed veterinarian who prepared
his needle. He collapsed, out of an arid old age,
onto the tiled floor as if it were a cold, deep creek

at the secret heart of a soft meadow, trickling up
to soothe his parched belly. Dear Lady, let this
faithless prayer (and the five dollar bill I've stuffed
in the poor box) atone for his death at my hands,

and for the City's common pit of dead animals
I had him thrown in when I refused to pay
for more. Ask him to forgive my unforgivable
disloyalty and return to my dreams, the way

he so often came when he was alive; sleek, young
and powerful as he was that long ago Fourth of
July, leaping to catch lit firecrackers in his teeth,
shaking his head and laughing at the explosions.

At the Last Judgment

everyone will know everything.
Sinners and saints will be amazed at
how little they ever suspected.
Until then, guard your murky heart.
God has good reasons to forgive
what husbands and wives can't.

Nicotine

Is the skeleton flashing
like a heartbeat
through the body.
It's the satisfaction

of knowing that life
like a good meal
will eventually turn to shit.
Your life as well as mine.

Smoke's what we do with our
hands and our mouths to
keep them away from
each other. It's the nipple

we suck instead of fucking. And—when
life suddenly grins—the hot breath
we lick like spun sugar between
screws to savor our scent.

Every twelve year old who tears
the cellophane knows without
reading the warning: Cigarettes
are war, courage, luck. Tobacco,

like fine brown clay wrapped
in white elegance, reminds us
of our place and that flesh
is a candle. Reminds us that

fools have the right to insist
on striking the match themselves.

And Yet Another Resurrection . . .

It doesn't matter.
Easter comes to everyone,
those who keep Lent,
and those who stagger into April
with Christmas still
reeking on their breath.

The dead Greeks, who believed in
inescapable Aphrodite, believed
that in silky spring her whisper's
impossible to deny:
those who willingly follow

she leads gently
into her thorny dreams,
those who foolishly resist, discover
the nightmare of their
lives. Sweet or bitter
anarchy. The season's

the same. Another new voice, a sudden
mouthful of rose petals, clothes
that won't ever fit
until they're torn to rags

Dream Politics

Humane

is a strange concept. A word we take visiting to some
very dark places. The CIA practices humane interrogation.
Lethal injection is humane—as were the electric chair

and the long drop, before. The Humane Society gasses our
unwanted pets. The ancients were being human as well
as humane when they sacrificed a pound or so of

ritually slaughtered beef to the nectar nourished gods,
hoping to entice heaven to share and absolve
carnivorous guilt. Our slaughterhouses with their

conveyers, pulleys and killing machines are inhumane
but efficient. As are cats who play for hours with their
prey, just to savor their own cruel saliva.

But are they unhuman as well? The really big, wild
cats, after all, don't toy with their kill. Hunger
is too insistent. It's the sleek, Purina fed housecat

that revels in torturing the starved trembling mouse,
the peeping crippled sparrow. And the ordinary
guy with a bit of a Budweiser gut who patiently

chomps a pizza on his gently rocking boat and nurses
his excitement—waiting for the nibble of a really big one,
the still ignorant pull on the barely visible line:

The kind of fish we all want, the kind that fights
futilely against the hook in its craw
and runs again and again from him,

full of hope, then ever so slowly,
losing hope. ever so slowly reeled
in by his brand new, slick equipment.

Power

So the thieves are back with their cynical smiles—
what they never earned they just take with a wink.
It's the same old arrogant game: What's good
for them is best. They wave the bible to proclaim
the rules and praise the Lord who created fools

Jack

When Jack had Judith Exner brought around back
to the little maid's room in the big White House,
he always made sure to do the job, three, four times
before relaxing on the pillow with his cigar.
He liked to tickle her nipple just so slightly,
nothing too blatant, while he set out to learn
what he wanted to know. "That old pervert, Giancana.
Tell me again, how he tries to do it to you.

I want to hear. I want to know everything.
I'll bet he's got some juicy things to say about Bobby, eh?
Just stick it out a little longer. Doesn't that feel good?
Don't I make it up to you? I just need to know a little more.
Momo will get what's coming to him, don't worry . . . Listen,
Judy, that stuff you hear about Marilyn, don't pay any attention.
That's all bullshit. Why would I want a fluff like that? "

Fifteen years later, a new president—a man of Jack's
very own party—but not very clear on the concept—
assured us that he, like the rest of us, suffered
from unrequited lust—and that he'd never, ever, tell a lie.
Hearing this, all across America we slept peacefully in our
marital beds. But in Arlington, the earth quaked, as Jack
sputtered and turned, over and over, in his smoking grave.

In the Fourth Year
of the Emperor's Glorious

adventure, we discovered the honey
bees were quietly deserting our orchards.
Then, almost as if they weren't there,
young amputees began appearing

on the streets. Sullen exiles on crutches,
too proud to question, at a loss
to explain—the Emperor's
broken toys. By the fourth

year the war was long won,
but we still couldn't deal
with the spoils rotting in the sun.

While wasps and flies and soldier
boys buzzed like bright ideas
in the Emperor's brainless skull.

There's That Strange Recurring Dream

The government of sneak thieves has finally
been overthrown by a revolution
of murderers. Our children
are in the streets, stalking their prey.
People are numb. They can't
make simple choices, can't decide
whether to go to work, drive
to the store. They cling
to their houses like trout behind
rocks in a winter river.

We watch the new leaders on television:
Master Sergeant Waldo, Monsignor Kelly,
the ascetic Police Captain Striker.
Each is wary of the others.
They agree on the points of order
without smiling. We realize
it doesn't so much matter what's forbidden.
It's only important to know that all
penalties have now been reduced to death.

We lie here, naked, on the covers,
washed by the flickering silver light,
titillated by their static voices.
All non-procreative sex is now banned,
they agree, and our puckering
middle aged bodies are dazzled
by the forgotten excitement of mortal sin.

Joseph and Magda in the Bunker

Three generations past that other,
1945, May day. Listening to Shirer's sad
audiobook in the muted park. Sunlight

almost embarrassed by its warmth. Two
pond geese, each standing on one leg
like question marks. What deity blessed
those bastards with such lovely children?

Joseph and Magda Goebbels, who chose
not to live without Hitler. But, first,
poisoned their Helga, Hedwig, Heidrun,
Holdine, Hildegard and Helmut.

Helga, the eldest, may have suspected;
distinct bruising was noted around her
mouth. Were the others already asleep
from the pinch of their morphine injections?

All six, ages two to twelve, laid out in pajamas
for the Soviets to find, ribbons in the dear
girls' hair. Did their parents think they
were cheating the victors of their spoils?

Childless Hitler did the same with
his joyous Shepherd, Blondi.
Cynics might say Adolf was just testing
the cyanide Eva would soon consume.

But the mere thought of killing blameless
animals had long since shocked that butcher
into vegetarianism. He loved his dog.
And loved his Fräulein Effie, too.

The paired geese peck idly at insects
and preen. In the weeds, shadowy
carp mouth their omnivorous way.

And wriggling up from the mud to
the little island, lovestruck turtles
lay their innocent, reptile eggs.

The Jogger

Mornings, running along the quiet
paths, that's when you can most
often see the animals. Those
strange, dead, bloated things.

Some resemble some kind of cat,
but of course, so different. Some
with pink, fingerlike claws, misshapen
bodies; some with green fur.

Once, I think I saw a fleshy rodent the size
of a young Rottweiller some ten feet
from the path in a clump of weeds.
I didn't stop to look too closely.

The City maintains the paths. By mid afternoon
they've been picked up, tossed in the garbage truck.
It seems natural they should all be dead.
They're so malformed. So individual.
Animals without a species.

On clear mornings, running through that
park, you can sense almost every fold in the Santa
Cruz mountains. The dark trees and gullies, the creases

in between the rocks; those secret places where the earth
experiments, makes her patient adjustments, quietly begins
to form the creature that's going to feed on man.

Mother Eve and Father

Adam, whose first born was a murderer—
who murdered for religion just like
any religious maniac—to protect
his personal pipeline to God . . .

How quickly the paradise of toddling
brothers turned to horror in that family
none of us can escape. Like so many
parents who've lost their children, did our

first parents stop touching each other?
Did they withdraw into their solitary
separate failures? Each with their

own bitter prayers. Was God
shocked too? At seeing them
scrabbling in the desert rocks

when they should have still been
sipping cool waters under the palms.
It wasn't God who'd made them leave.
But how could He reach them now?

To make them realize they themselves
were the garden, the snake, the apple,
the sneering angel, and the dream gone bad.

Martyrs

In Stonewall Jackson's eyewitness account, old
John Brown was made to stand—white-hooded
and noosed, for fifteen minutes on the scaffold—
while they maneuvered the solemn troops.

When the trap finally sprang, he strangled
for another like time, arms pinioned at the elbows,
hands sprung up helpless at ninety degrees,
clenching, unclenching . . .

Nothing really botched or unintended. The rope—
as Major Jackson's sharp eye noted—was
measured for the standard four foot drop. In
the Commonwealth's eyes, humane. Punishment

he certainly had coming. Better, when you think about
it, than three hours dangling on the Cross. Better than a young
French girl burnt alive for communing with angels. Easier
than Father Edmund Campion, drawn and quartered for

love of the scheming Pope. Brown's was a predictable, Southern
end. Look what the old Yankees once did to witches. Look
at the chaos the new Yankees were itching to sow. The planters
could smell their steel shackled world, squirming with rage.

But politics and the age aside: martyrs lack all
common sense. The worst offer their blood in a bloody cause.
And if others simply decline to lie—none of them are pure.
To their inquisitors, even the meekest are angry lambs.

What's gained but the hallelujah of judicial suicide...
Centuries earlier, Galileo Galalei may have been
agonizing along these lines when he bowed, recanted,
then retired to his garret window to sigh and mutely circle

an undeniable sun along with the slow twirling earth.
Did he escape his miserable fate? Or just suffer
nine more penitential years, choking on the
bonfired smoke of his smoldering work?

No one ever wrote a hymn to him or marched in
battle to its step. But in the Florence museum where
his papers repose, his right hand's desiccated middle finger
is preserved under glass, a stubborn relic raised to glory.

Hell

Imagine—if you can—the eternal
loneliness a single almighty God might
feel: Creating universe upon universe,
species beyond any species' imagination.

Knowing all the while they're just
wishes feeding on whims.
Imagine the insanity and shriek
that being God implies:

Incapable of dying, unable to sleep.
But of course you're human,
so the best you can do

is imagine yourself as God.
And that's where
hell begins.

In Ovid the Flaying

of Marsysas begins in *medias res*.
Why?—the shocked satyr screams—
aghast at the god's senseless
cruelty—*are you skinning me?*

Apollo, that serene force, smiles
while the flensers continue.

And the slippery innards of the great
howling creature spill out like worms
writhing in sudden daylight.

No song is worth this, the bleeding wretch
manages to gasp. These are his last spoken words.

At least, as Ovid tells the story.
But it's an old tale he's telling.
Everyone knew how it began:

Athena's idly tossed aside double-*aulos*
glittering in the meadowgrass. Marysas's
innocent joy as he puffs his cheeks and hears

something wholly new: his own deepest
being bubbling in that numinous
instrument. An irresistibly personal hymn

only his loving goatish lips can coax from
the heavenly flute. Never before melodies
that couldn't fail to impress the placid Lord
of poetry, music and sunlight as he ambled
by and suggested a little game.

Not really a contest, more a sort of duet?
Marsyas would pipe, Apollo could
pluck his lyre, maybe hum a bit?
But rather than perform together in
harmony, they'd alternate verses. And whoever
pleased the leggy pasture lazing Muses more

would treat the loser to whatever pleased him.
What was Marsyas thinking? Certainly, not
what seething, insulted divinity had in mind.

Was it any comfort his meadow-blood clarified
and wept as it seeped beneath the grass—then
welled and flowed anew as it became
the purest spring in Phrygia?

—*for Neeli*

There's Something Unexplainably Oppressive About

this speechlessness, as if it weren't enough
for me to keep quiet, as if I've been assigned
nasty keepers—a persecutor
who strolls into my cell
four or five times a day
to remind me in his memorized English—
"No talk. No words. No speaking
allowed." But as he leaves the cell-block, the steel

doors ringing in the air, the guard's fear
lingers like cologne. As if they know
the simplest language can destroy these walls.
Know, even if they were to tear out
my tongue, shatter my cellmates' ears,
our fingertips dancing in code
would recite the story of the resurrection
and the life. It's the inexplicable
illusion of solitude that keeps me silent.

Bankruptcy

It began—in the 1500s—as a convenience for creditors.
A sort of truce between predators, so that the fastest,
the most vicious couldn't just swagger in like a lion
and carry off the carcass with a roar. The purpose

of the procedure was to freeze the shivering
debtor in place, while his bankers negotiated
their nibbling rights. The wretch had little
to say. No preference, beyond a morbid curiosity,

as to who took which bite where. And after
the lawyers finished. After the lenders washed
their hands, disgusted at the slim pickings:
the court would often record its frustration

by ordering the Bankrupt's ear sliced off.
A permanent credit report, a warning to anyone
with money—Don't lend your money here.
A caution to anyone who borrowed—Don't fail.

But, of course, we all fail. Our teeth fail, our eyes
fail, our livers, our marriages and hearts. Dementia lurks
like a demon and nothing succeeds in the end.

Why would those with eyes to see
resist their credit cards—their platinum
road to ruin? A vacation in Rome, a wedding at the Ritz,

a year of nothing but the best. We've overthrown the aristocracy.
We live in the republic of the free now, the democracy
of bliss where the lamb eats the lion's lunch.

When bankruptcy pours the wine,
only fools postpone joy. Justice is elusive.
But mercy is always within our grasp.

Escape

Sentiment is the wall with spacious,
lovely windows that keeps
me from running out the door.
I want to toss a
few kisses and scatter
my goodbyes. I want

a jungle, but my keepers insist
on champagne. I'd slide twenty
floors down the banisters, but, I confess
I'm hypnotized by the winking eyes
they've painted on their desk drumming
fingernails. I don't belong, I confess.

And at my late age, I confess I don't
want to slop out my confession
to any goddamn priest. The way
the suburbs want something better
for themselves, I want a city

I can love. Fog. Church bells. Hour bells.
Unscalable buildings. Fire escapes. A row
of dim orange windows. A disappearing moon.
Footsteps. Voices. Sirens. A running
gutter full of plots.

Ancestors

Depression Album

In those photographs it's always winter,
even shirtless in the sun, the skinny
kids with bowl cropped hair wince
at an invisible wind.
Riffle the pages to any one
and, under the gloss, a persistent gray
smudges your fingers like coal soot.
No meat left on the bone, everyone a failure,
and once you begin to shiver in that numb
cold, you're lost. You wouldn't
want to go where they are or where
they're going next. Our fathers
and mothers who changed so
much once the worst was over.

Fireflies

—*for Dick Grossman's 50th birthday*

Standing in line in the Silicon Valley cafe, waiting
for the spike orange haired sweetie to get around
to flashing her undivided attention
on my tired hunger, I distract myself by counting
out how few days are left in the century

I used to take for granted. I'm barely
listening when, as quietly as May, the digitally remastered
voice of Billie Holiday at twenty slips out of the elegant
speakers, as naked as a kiss. And just like that, the dazzling
chrome and plastic room is blessed with a shower of gardenias.

In the teens and twenties, when they finally electrified
the last sleepy farm towns, they say something shy deserted our
nights. Not the glow, but the sudden dark whisper that candles
honor, the invisible blossom fireflies pollinate. Is this
where the fireflies disappeared to?

Corruption on Earth

In 1501—or was it 1502? I can't remember.—Cesare Borgia
gave a surprise party for his father, the Pope, and his sister, Lucretia.
It was a mild autumn, and on an impromptu stage under the great
arbor, fifty prostitutes danced, demurely dressed, and then,
danced naked for half an hour before dispersing to crawl
under the dining tables to beg for chestnuts.

Perhaps Cesare thought the revelry might cheer his sister
who was still mourning—though she'd be damned if she'd
let them see it—her treacherous husband those bastards
had strangled. She'd really loved that eager, ignorant,
frightened boy. But politics was business after all... And
did the chronicler mention Julia Bella, the comfort

of Pope Alexander's declining years? Was she at the party?
Five years earlier, when he was sixty three, and she was still
the fourteen year old he'd married to one-eyed Orso Orsini
he wrote to remind her he was the Pope as well as her
lover. And if he ever caught her in bed with her husband,
he'd excommunicate and damn her soul for all eternity.

A nasty family. But history reminds us violent Cesare was
the most exemplary of princes; that Lucretia grew gradually
old and repentant, and died a near saint; that Alexander
was devoted to the Virgin to the point of superstition,
and—as corpulent as any well fed tenor—would sing
the Christmas mass in a voice so lovely it brought tears
to the crystal hearts of the pious. The righteous
may like to imagine their Borgias roasting in hell with Hitler,

but Christians should forgive and, personally, I'm touched
by the image of old Alexander roasting chestnuts, sipping his
Sangiovese, waiting for the party to start and wondering
what that sly son of his had up his sleeve for the evening.

"What the hell's the point of being pope,"
I can hear him muttering, "if you can't indulge
your own little sins, as well as the sins of others?"

Hemingway at Sixty

In his sleep, he hears something burrowing under the house,
scraping at the grout in the tiled floor. Then wakes to find blood
spots on the pillow. Despite the sun, he just can't seem to get warm.
Even so, he writes. But there's no longer room for the old demons

on the page. The mouths of the cabinet ministers and Guardia
kneeling in the mud have gaped too wide. And he's getting smaller
each week, each hour. His only hope is to lock them squirming
in the cellar. Who would the butchered slaughter if they could?

We marveled at the virtue, the humanity,
the optimism of those last works. At how he'd
mellowed and matured. We never noticed how tiny

he'd become in his skin. How fragile his eyes
seemed to be. How little of himself he'd come to own.
How the locks were being picked and the door was opening.

Casanova at Dux

In July, he dreams of
a century of snow. Of frost
as stunning as the sun, glittering
like a knife in
the eye. But by August,
the landscape turns ambivalent.
Rain and the hint of rain

whisper like lovebirds,
then hiss like fucked out cats.
In September, his fever, cautiously,
begins to toy with the idea—
and then all at once October
bursts free. A millennium
of silver. A moon full of clever tongues.

What's left but to, helplessly,
tell the damn story.

Wine

To understand, you have to imagine what we're just
beginning to suspect: What it must have been like
drifting through light years of emptiness in that
spaceship, nearly a million years ago.

But at least they still were breathing the oxygen
of their receding home: those gold forests that
seem so familiar, so impossible; the brilliant blue
cities, the sacred towers of our elusive dreams.

When they crashed, it was on a planet that was—
for the most part—ice. Their harsh new world.

They tried to maintain their simple religion,
but how long did it take to realize the gods
here were cruel and diverse? The grizzly,
the tiger, the marauding leathery birds would
never accept them. Except as food.

And scavenging, warily inhaling,
surviving as best they could,
it wasn't long before they saw what this
desolate world would do to them.

They began to age and die so quickly. Their thousand
year lifetimes accelerated. They were becoming what
we now call—human. A painful condition they
really didn't care to explore.

Only generations later did the castaways
begin to suspect the possibility of a thaw.
And it was later, much later, that finally, snaking
its tentative way through the still naked
loam, the awakening grape beckoned to them.

The way any lonely, natural god might, the eager
vine decided to teach these hopeless wanderers
its secrets. Even if that treason to its dark jealous
root meant it would be mute forever more.
With wine they began to understand their sullen
adopted home, began to feel her core of warmth.
They made themselves a little stupid, like the animals.
Knew why dogs were happy. Began to believe
they could be brothers to the bear. Began to call
the earth, "Mother." And to think of themselves

again as a race of poets, adventurers, priests.
They blessed the wine, called it "invisible sun"
and "blood of our blood", took heart and began
to plant and cultivate, ferment and nurture, and buy
and sell this poison and absolute necessity of life.

Since You Asked Why...

Poets are children until they die
and wine brings Christmas every night.

Reincarnation

In earliest childhood, in the crib still
digesting the fear of your lingering last death—
did you scream? When she weaned you from
the nipple and led you to the table

did your mother have any idea
how much terror still lurked in the devouring
little mouth you could only appease
with a new, un-clotted language?

Now, just once in a while, at night
in those dreams your lovers report—
dead to the world but talking bolt upright:

What is it you're so urgently describing
in what foreign tongue, not in the slightest
aware that no one understands?

Asylum

All I can remember about him is
the last time we visited him, but I'm
sure there must have been visits before:

I remember him being so familiar.
An especially gentle, foreign man, wistful
in what feels like October sunlight, sitting
close to him on the green bench, listening
to his voice try to become precise then
slip back into confusion as he tries to speak
English to me ... Then I remember them laughing

when my grandmother tried to translate.
He was warning us about the nuts, the insane.
The place was full of them and we shouldn't
shake hands with them, shouldn't bring
glass bottles, anything they could make
into a weapon. How some of them were vicious.

We'd brought him whiskey, but he wouldn't touch it.
I think he explained—he was honestly trying to—
do what was right this time—achieve something?
I'm not sure what he said, but he seemed to be
immensely calm, as if he'd made a decision, was just
marking time. But I so distinctly remember
him lifting me, hugging me to his stubbled cheek,

making a big show of acting as if I were the only
one who understood his strange sadness.
So that I was scared he might tell me
something horrid, some secret—and I pulled away.

After the picnic, while he and my grandmother
gossiped, my father took me for a walk
around the place. Told me about the mad people
locked in cages like the zoo, too violent, too
helpless to let walk loose. How some

would have to be tied in jackets to keep them
from biting off their fingers, and others
would simply stand in corners, not weeping
not moving, secretly breathing, would piss
down their legs like babies.
He made it seem very real, because—although
it couldn't be true—I still remember moving
past a row of cages as if we were in a dark
lion house, holding my father's hand and
listening to shrieks and giggling,

But all these memories just seem to exist
like unconnected words from a time when
I was almost someone else, hardly
four, or five, when I could still speak Polish.

Casanova Redux

Odi et amo. Quare id faciam fortasse requiris.
Nescio, sed fieri sentio, et excrucior.
—Catullus

1795
"Sensing I'd come to an age where I was no longer
attractive to women," he confesses—"I resolved to
content myself with the services of an honest prostitute..."
Even so—nearing the end of the grand *Histoire*—hope

mutters while lust broods. Has his unquenchable
muse really left? In a disquieting four
a.m. dream, death—a bundled nun with
bad breath—tries to kiss him. "Loss,"

he begins to write, "is inseparable
from love, sex just mortality's angel face."
Tired stuff, he thinks, as he crosses
out the lines. As old as Catullus.

There's a certain anger lurking
here. At who? At what?
Odi et amo—the eager crucifix
of love, as inescapable at seventy as
it was at seventeen...

Gisele is circling a defeated
thirty. Already dumpy, a tooth missing on
her left side. That hint of coming roughness
at her throat and breasts. But her calculating smile

wins his iffy interest. Once a week he spends
an afternoon with her. Telling her stories she pretends
to believe. Luxuriating in her laundry soap smell
and the involuntary little shudders he still knows

how to coax, despite herself . . . One day,
strolling the city, he stumbles across
Gisele being dragged off by a bailiff she
lacked the funds to bribe. The old man's

walking stick flashes like a sword
in the squat official's face. "The Count,
my friend and patron, will clap
you in irons for this. Let her go."

And she's released to Casanova's
comforting arms. Her real tears the
sudden water of life to him. But
the realization that—at best—he

may have earned a small discount
stings like a chancre. "Who'd have
guessed when I was a lion, that all
that proud hunger could beg like this?

I disgust myself, and can't
help myself. Don't ask why,
that's just the way it is. But why,
why does that ache still glow?"

Angel Rain

Do you remember Hemingway's sad heroine
who was afraid of the rain she said
she saw herself dying in it and didn't
Mozart and think of poor Chopin
in love on Mallorca feeling the storm churn
like an icy ocean at the bottom
of a well in his shivering lungs.

It's only earth that loves rain, that sucks
it like an angel's kiss into its greedy, dirty
mouth. It's only earth that teaches us
to listen for the almost invisible sigh of feathers
against the air, of wings shaking off water
like fear. It's only when clouds
hide their hearts from the sun that angels
dare to remember how sweet it was to be a bitter
animal astonished by their sudden grace.

Homage to Ithaca

Penelope

When she heard the rumors he'd finally
be coming home—months away, a long way off
—did she sense how broken hearted
he'd want to be: Circe, clinging
to his dreams like tangled hope.
Calypso lingering on his tongue.
One-eyed Cyclops blindly bellowing
on the distant wind. A man like that

wouldn't look forward to much
but his fire. The old dog snoring
at his feet. His winecup full of an
insistent sea of voices, ocean moonlight,
dark water. Tied to his
chair like a mast by memories,
floating through a mist of illiterate
goddesses, scheming witches and useless war.

Is that when she opened the gates, put
flowers in her hair and invited
the young noble toughs to stay?
Flirting with one, then another, feeling
this one's tattooed muscles, dropping a dirty
remark to the blond with the razor spear.
Perched, resplendent as Helen, at the head of the drunken
table, is that when she dispatched her urgent
welcome: Your home is waiting to be conquered.

Telemachus

For the boy it was a bit
more desperate. Was he fourteen,
fifteen when he realized the score—
the inevitable in store for him?

The stepson prince of an occupied country.
Once the claimant claimed his bride,
Telemachus would certainly disappear.
A knife in the back. a sudden

garrote in an alley. His skinny-kid's
corpse sailing away in a sack full of stones.
The ungrateful runaway who broke his mother's heart.
Except she certainly knew. Wisdom

ran deep in that family.
So when Athena flittered down
and became an old man, it was no surprise.

They listened. Get out while you can, she
whispered. Don't ever come back here
without your father.

I Was Nobody

When that proud god's barbarous
son, who cracked men's skulls like
eggshells to drink their brains, asked
me—I didn't want to have a name.
I wanted to crawl, slither, squirm

through some crevice into nameless
nothingness. I wanted to be as
small as could be and still be.
Too tiny to see, too quiet for
salivating tongues to notice.

Not that hushed moment the
shivering white ox, sprinkled
with barley rests in just before
it's hammer-stunned and the bronze
blade slits its veins.

Not the ear-pricked stillness that
pauses the thirsty stag, wondering
what else might be lurking near
the trickling stream.

I was more shameful prey: a piglet
too paralyzed to squeal, a hoarse
rooster complicitly shedding
its panicked feathers.

No One—oh gods—if I was No One,
no one would hurt me. Everything
else was just a trap.

On the filthy floor
of Cyclop's blood slick cave,
I only wanted to be whatever
it was I was before being squeezed
into this carnivorous world.

So, doing what had to be done and
blinding that drunken one-eyed
prick was like being reborn, naked
alone and screaming

Odysseus, Odysseus, and don't
you or your damned father-god
forget the name that will
outlive you both.

Circe

He slept with her because, as Hermes warned, it
was too dangerous not to. And then, again and
again for a year, because she was a slow, warm

dark tide in a golden August sea. They
went from "Your face looks like a god's
when you come" to "It's your flawed humanity

I love," to "You're flawed." Every bit as much
as summer, winter has its reasons. He left
when it became too dangerous not to.

The Sirens

What surprised him—so helpless and expectant—
was that the sound was something else than sound.
A sense of sunlight in the ear, a fragrance
that could only be heard and then a wing
and the utter joy of flight. As much beyond music
as harmony transcends speech. A heartleap
into a resonance so god-like he suddenly
knew what it was the gods worshipped.
And all this from the tonsils of three
wretched crones who sang as mindlessly as
spiders weave. Hunger is treacherous.

Being a Poet

Homer imagined how the dead might be invoked:
by digging a pit and tempting them
into daylight with the sweet taste of blood.

He imagined the lost might prophesy, might
know—not only what was and what is,
but—things still yet to be.

And did the tale-spinner hope (as everyone
does) he might somehow avoid his own
dark trip into those ant caves where
millions upon millions patiently work

preparing a place for each of us, watching
our brightness from the shadows?
Countless, breathless eyes
caught up in our every word.

And Then There Was Tiresias

Who, in a complicated story full of copulating snakes,
became a woman for seven years, then changed back to
being a man.

To quote Teresias, who had every reason to know:

"... insofar as sexual pleasure,
the woman's measure
is nine times that of the man's"

Of course, Hera plucked out his eyes
for saying what he said.
Any woman who thinks a man
gives her more than he takes,
has to be blind.
And any man who
believes those helpless moans
is being led by his blind-eyed worm.

Kalypso

Hermes, quietly, slipped
out of the forest one day with a wink
and a message from Circe.
"Your cousin wanted you to know,"
he smiled. "There's more than a chance
he'll come this way. Don't pass him up."

"What is it Circe sees in mortals, Hermes?"
The messenger god coughed, then mimicked
Circe's lazy, curious voice: "Like the rest of them,
he has that fascinating fragrance of death.
But he's smarter than most. He sees
it clearly, and he doesn't whine."

"You know, Hermes, (Circe said this)
we gods can't stomach a bite of flesh,
still we drool for the smoke
of the cookfire. Human ass
is always on fire and it's
the sweetest burnt offering."

When I asked Hermes what *he* thought,
he shrugged. "Everyone to their own taste.
I do my share to help humans,
I don't think I need to fuck them.
Lonely goddesses, on little islands,"
he smiled, "are a different story."

But even with his clever prick and hands
dear, sweet Mercury seemed
somehow lacking and distracted.

... It was just a week or so later
that Ulysses staggered out of the pounding
surf: parched, speechless, and blind with

salt, trembling, like a soon to be sacrificed
lamb. I must have been only
a gentle blur to him as I guided him
to my little house in the pines.
I let him suck on a sponge soaked
in clear spring water, then washed him

and watched over him while he slept.
Slowly, with ambrosia and honey and
small cups of wine mixed with rosewater,
I nursed him back to himself.

There wasn't any hurry. I wasn't
Circe—I know how to take my time.

Weeks later, when he was really
ready, when he could hardly wait, I took
his dark curly head between my morning-pink
thighs—and then he knew. He would never
have done—that—with any human woman. And
not with Circe, either, I was sure.

Circe had him for a year.
I lost track of time, but it must
have been at least five
years before he stopped following me
from room to room and began to wander
off on his own. Even then,

at first it was only to gather flowers
for me, or to collect his thoughts so
he could remember a song.
I have so much time, it's hard
to pay attention, so I don't know
just when it was I stumbled upon him

behind the sea rocks, roasting three
plucked doves on a thin stick over
his little fire. I was too shocked
to let him see me, and kept myself hidden
in the trees. But that night, still keeping
my secret in our vine-canopied bed

I shocked myself again by screaming
in absolute delight as his smoky hands
caressed my fine white spine.
He came with such a helpless
pleading shiver that I realized he knew
I'd seen him eating the innocent flesh

and was simply waiting for my judgment.
I waited. I didn't have his urgent
human nerves. I waited to see if
he would kill again and when I smelled
the smoke and blood on his fingers, I still waited
just to see if he'd raise the subject.

After enough time passed to convince me
he'd be happy to live a lie forever,
I asked him to sleep apart from me for a night.
And in the morning, with a smile, I asked,
"Ulysses, isn't the ambrosia which keeps
you young and lets you live with me almost as

if you too were a god—isn't that enough for you?
Or is something else wrong between us?"
He was clever enough not to lie.
"I'm an animal," he said. "It can't be
changed. I'm sorry for the birds and rabbits.
Beyond that, I make no judgment."

He could never hurt me, but for the first time
I was a little frightened to be alone with him.
He'd slept at our door all night and had washed
in the spring. But, while there was no trace of smoke
or burnt flesh, he had a quiet, brooding fragrance
of old dried roses mixed with fresh earth, mushrooms

and acorns. I noticed how scarred and wood-like
the palms of his hands were and I realized
that whatever cautions he'd felt about Circe,
he had absolutely no fear of me. I let him
take me there on the grass. Rode under him
like an acrobat under a bull in the ring,

then, knelt shuddering on all fours
to pleasure him like a cow. I was never
more supple, delicate or submissive.
And after I'd drained all his power
he held me—I thought—like a precious
serving girl he'd slapped in a stupid rage.

Though I never asked him to stop,
I don't think he hunted much again.
But in the place of that conniving hunger,
he slowly developed an annoying habit of
sadness. He was, if anything, more solicitous
than he'd been since our first months. But still,

I could sense so much of him was elsewhere,
not listening. And I began to notice, after all
these years, that despite his diet of ambrosia
and my sacred caresses, he was developing
certain wrinkles, a fleshiness at the neck,
a, decidedly, middle aged stoop.

The morning he finally, sheepishly
asked if he might be allowed to go
home to die with his old wife—I thought—
"I've had the best of him. The rest
is nothing but loss. Better all at once
than watching this little by little."

So we built a nice little boat and I tied
my scarf around his neck. I felt quite
magnanimous, quite divine. It wasn't until
I saw how he skipped like a boy into the waves
and looked back laughing that I wondered:
Had I really been such a burden?

Nausicaa

She said she wanted Odysseus for a husband. An
arrangement her father was utterly willing to make.
But really, it was something more primal,

more hazardous to that peaceable realm. All
that year, puzzled, amnesiac moods kept
invading her. "Where was I before

I was here? How did I get here?"
This puny island at the edge of boring nowhere.
An ambitionless people, so unfond of conflict

and weapons, that they purposely
settled in a spot no one really cared about.
Petty traders, bribers of their enemies: The women

wove, the men—danced! Not a hero or poet among
them. "Was this why I was born?"

Every night, their little banquet. Her jowled, kinglet
daddy, his simple minded cow of a queen. Chewing
their stupid food, munching like toothy mules.

When the thirteen year old darling chasing her
errant ball crashed into the brine covered
castaway, all sinew and hunger, standing there

like some glittering Achilles in the mist eating sun,
and he asked—"Are you human or divine, young lady?"—
he was the sudden answer to her brooding question:

"Who am I, who are these people? What did they do
with my real mother, my real father?

Argus

Some say Homer embellished an older story—
perhaps the tale that Nausicaa, grown up to be a poet,
spun—a woman's tale that praised a constant wife,
a belabored husband—a man of many chaste sorrows.

It was Homer who wove in the nightmares
and dreams, the lotus eaters, the monsters,
and perfumed islands under a naked new moon.

And Homer who imagined faithful Argus:

At journey's end, still disguised
as an old beggar, but finally face to face
with Penelope, our hero's eyes danced with joy
at her benevolent, glowing eyes. He was pleased

with her graciousness to the duplicitous
traveler who assured her Odysseus would
soon be home to claim his own. She'd aged

well, he noticed, barely a wrinkle. still somewhat
slim, just a tiny bit gray. But he had to admit
there were certain moments that were

none of her business, he wouldn't have
traded for twenty years of wedded bliss.
Odysseus was at peace as he left Penelope.

       ... It was the old dog Argus

dragging his arthritic hips, his hound's
heart leaping to heaven as he collapsed
in the ecstatic scent of his lost master....

Watching that pitiful cur die, the whole long
watery exile screamed and became stone.
His wandering rage turned to iron. Something
essential snapped into place. With thighs

like trees, shoulders sinewed with oak root,
he strode into the banquet hall, his clever
hands flexing for the leather and bow.

When I Reach the Point Where Telemachus

hangs the women, I feel ashamed
for his bloodthirsty father who ordered
the slaughter and for Telemachus,
who chose to sadistically strangle them all
on one dancing rope.
But most of all, I'm ashamed for

Homer, who knowing so much,
surely knew better. They were sluts
who slept with the enemy, he tells us.
They got no more than their stupidity deserved.
Couldn't he have—just as easily—used
the opportunity to remind us

that cruelty to the helpless is our most monstrous trait?
And, then, when they disembowel and cut
off the nose and ears and hands and feet of the treacherous
steward, I know things have gotten out of hand. What
human purpose does any of this, almost Jehova-like,
retribution serve? And I begin to suspect

the cat and mouse savagery of divine intervention.
Who else but the subtle and unforgiving goddess of wisdom,
who—chastely, but no less than her rural sisters—
loved Ulysses above all mortal men for
the clarity of his deceptive eyes
and the sudden logic of his violence?

Poseidon

In the end, it was the god of earthquakes
and the sea Odysseus could never make
peace with. The deity who turns

the solid ground beneath our feet
to running sand. Who tempts
us with calm waters to travel just

a little further, until it's too late.
The divine power who had no mercy
on the merciful sailors who
finally brought our wanderer safely home.

Who made their ship a drowning
rock. Who raged and mourned his
monstrous cannibal son, but reveled
in the helplessness of men.

Pork

And thou, Oh swineherd Eumaeus—
the only one in all the volumes
the singer spoke directly to:
Was all this for you?

The unappeasable gods,
the foaming journey, all those good
men lost to slippery fame and bad behavior.
The wandering son and the wandering
father, needing just you, *oh swineherd*
Eumaus, to see into each other like mirrors.

Of course you begin to glow, but wonder
why such poetic honor should come
to someone so humble? Could it be,
you ponder, that the time may be
finally arriving when the last shall be
first on this earth? The delicious way

his subtle voice suddenly wafts
you into the wild story like oven smoke:
And it's you, you, *oh swineherd Eumaeus*,
you, who in the end saves their bacon
at the slaughter of the gluttonous.

And your chest swells while you smile
never suspecting you're just a blur
in nearsighted old Homer's
book-ruined eyes. That it's the platter
in your greasy fingers he's trying
to tempt within reach.

Departures

That Day at the Met

what really whispered to me were not
the remnants of their useless gods,
but those sad, minus fourth century, Greek
grave stelae: The deceased ritually seated

as if hearing his or her prognosis for the first stunned
time. The small group of friends, family, usually one
in particular—the most stricken?—holding the hand
of the departed in quiet solidarity. In one tableau, an

unmistakable twin brother. Has any of this
ever made sense to us?

        ... Abandoned lines from decades ago in an almost
discarded vacation notebook. So many since lost,
unforseen, gone. So many new reasons to again be so
haunted by the breath in those dead stones.

1999–2018

Broken April

What if this rain keeps on all summer. Someone
said it, could it be true?—the axis of the earth's

just shifted, slightly. And for the rest of our lives
there'll be rain. Suppose

this is just the beginning of the next great era:
The age of sadness (the kind of sadness there's

no answer for except dreams). Don't even
attempt it, don't try to understand

these mud brown clouds with your mind
—that helpless organ. The rain

is what roots you.
Death only happens once in a lifetime,

but your time revolves around it
like an invisible sun.

In Memory...

Death: The thief within the body
who wants to steal our blood.
But does it just run through his fingers
the way time does through ours? Is
he any less astonished than we are
when our heartbeats escape?

A Prayer for My Mother's Death

As if awakening.
As if it were suddenly May.
The way in which, in even the worst
nightmare, you simply remember
yourself, and smile and open your eyes
to a room that's been gently invaded
by an immense and curious sky.

And if, as sometimes happens
when we dream too deeply,
you're still pinned firmly to your bed
by white, muscled wings: Let the morning
take you into its own lazy dream.

My Demented Father Enters His 90th Year

After weeks of bitter insomnia,
you finally collapse and begin
to dream of the sacred forest and huge
thorn trees that scream all night.

Burglars, sent by your starved dead
wife to steal your hidden breath,
rummage the bedside drawers. But
you've already ... slipped into the wood

through the old cracked bark ... begun to swim
with the dark pulsing sap into the tunneling
taproot and the blind greed for earth and the diamond

of dazzling light at the core where all of us
always live. That frightening place, the blinding
flash, the eye that can't bear our touch.

January, Chicago

Even at the hollow core of winter:
Resonance. The wind within
answering the bitter chill with

its own dark, hungry tongue. Ice
weeping under the arc lights.
And the sun avoiding a cold frightened

world. If—despite everything—
there'll be spring: It will have to be
despite ourselves. Will have to bring

its own helplessness out of the insulated
mud. Its own trapped panic whistling
like a scream in a voice too strangled

to hear. Its own heartbeat. Its own blood. Its own
small fingers to lace between our own.

Park Benches

Arranged this way in front of the empty bandstand
in the fog, they're a convocation of ghosts each with its
own ID tag—the plaques sold by the forever needy City
to mourners abandoned by their dead.

Mother, father, sister, wife, child, husband:
each name inscribed in a brass sodality of sorrow,
whispering to the deaf, brash strollers who sit and ignore
the shocked begging mouths of a speechless wound.

But they're beyond that now; internees imprisoned
in endless snow, or wincing in a sudden desert of wind
and dust. Their names are all they've left behind, coins

from the turned out pockets of the condemned.
They lived once, they'll always live; but always
hungry as anything that's born will always be.

All Souls Day, 2008

Heaven

For me, it would have to be very much
like earth—green, troubled, insatiable.
Suspended between fire and night. Circling
its brooding choice. But it would be such

a heavenly earth. A sleeping planet, stunned
the way all earth's creatures are stunned when
sleep numbs their bodies to play. The way
the ant and mathematician both dream in their

prisons, the next life might be a drowsy earth—
an earth content to just dream about heaven.
A winter dream, a dream of seeds winking quietly

at the stars, whispering patience to an insistent
moon. An earth that remembers and forgets
and remembers, again and again.

Two Poems for Al Masarik, d. 2015.

All Saints Morning

A lazy, open door Saturday.
The sly, Chinese waitress quietly
flirts with you in painful English
while the cook chops vegetables for the soup.

You flirt with the bacon on your plate.
Your bacon—you think—has already flirted
with disaster, has no further
interest in any of this. But outside,

over the chimneys,
a black Halloween balloon set
free the morning after
sails like the risen Lazarus
into a blue, unsuspecting day.

Behind the bar, under spotless glasses,
the rich purple bottles lounge in rows
like squads of fat cops fingering
their nightsticks, waiting to
march you off to lunch.
And who's that walking past
the window on legs you can't
take your eyes off?

What's in the air that's so
helpless and promising? Everyone knows
about spring, but that snappy copper
headed woman's hair really needs
this hard, November, sidewalk light,
this especially anxious breeze to flutter

in that I don't mind winter come
get me way. Even in November, something
in the blood can't ever say no,
doesn't care you can't say why.

1986

For A Poet Who Lost his Voice

Before it took everything, time began to pilfer
one simple thing after another: how to set your
wrist watch, the inscrutable mechanics of lacing
your shoes. Scared, numb, slowly, your brain

forgot to eat or drink. Helpless, you went elsewhere.
But, well before that, your voice was the cruelest
departure. She could always whisper your secret
name. Until she began to stammer. The word

made flesh no more (that tongue of hushed kisses),
but an angel language mired in speechless
mud. What choice did she have but to leave

and weep? Your most unconsolable lover. You
never questioned your need for heaven, but who
can fathom heaven's hopeless need for us?

2015

Two Poems for Ann Menebroker, d. 2016

On the porch, skirt tucked, waiting for rain as the false

spring falters, you spot him sauntering up the walk:
A bit furtive. Vaguely foreign. Something primitive
and overly formal, in the way he climbs your
few steps, grimaces, then plunks himself next

to you on the swing. Something akin to
the aura, not an odor, of tobacco.
The kind of haircut they don't do over here.
A quiet little guy with no rhyme or reason

to him. As hard and compact as steel,
but his coldness somehow numbs your fear.
You smile, and when you go back in the house

to fix dinner, he follows as naturally
as your shadow. There's nothing to do
but set an extra plate.

Sitting there, he takes just one potato, one
mushroom and a carrot to be polite.
You never notice him eating, but
when you take up the dishes to wash,

the food is gone. He seems to like TV,
the news shows, an old PBS movie.
When it's time for bed, he nods as
you close your door. You don't care

where—or if—he sleeps. And in the morning,
he's sitting there in different, but
still strange clothes. Friends visit, come

and go, waiting for winter to end the drought.
They nod to him, he almost nods. And
everyone ignores him as best they can.

Then one day—it seems just yesterday he
first appeared—you find him packing
his small worn valise. He offers
an iron hand and winks: "We're going."

You make a point of not asking where.
"Don't look back", he warns. "Lot's wife
was frozen into salt." He shakes his head.
"Orpheus, lost his heart." He gestures

toward your suitcase. "I've already packed
your universe for you to bring along."
The bag is as light as air.

You close your eyes and lean
on him. And let him guide you,
desperately pretending to be blind.

2009

Non fui, fui, non sum . . .

Annie, Annie you're ashes now, who
once was blushing flesh. Is it a journey
or empty air? An old man mourning
an old, old friend really wants to know.

Sooner, I'm sure, than I'll like, I'll be
joining you. Will we babble like budgies
in a paradise of gossip, or stare, as secretive
as headstones? Where did our laughter live

until we met, that lifetime ago? Or before
we were even born, those million, trillion
years we weren't? There'll be millions,

trillions more when we aren't. But
Annie, for a little while, just talking
on this lost silly earth, we were.

2016

Disaster

What use are all these bargains
you'll never be able to keep?
And the gods aren't to be trusted either:
how else could such things happen?

Because divinity isn't everything
we're not, but everything we are
and can't sustain. The August
sunlight we can touch but never grasp.

Isn't that why we somehow believe
that at the speed of light
time stands still?

Unfortunates

What would you
give not to die? Your teeth,
your tonsils, your appendix?
Maybe an arm, your nose, your
larynx? (So that you'd have
to go around rasping through your leather throat hole.)
People so much like yourself
are doing it, every minute are just
cutting away parts of themselves. Feeding
death like an animal. It's just a
matter of will. You'd do
worse than pray to them (forget your
childish goddesses), the cancerous,
the crushed, the diseased. Sooner
or later you're going to become your disease.
Sooner or later you'll be one of those people you've
always cleanly cut out of your life, walked
away from so sternly.

Cemetery Strike

The contract expires, and almost in unison
all the gravediggers in the city
switch off their bulldozers. In the crematoriums,
the oven attendants turn off the gas
then blow out the pilots.
Even the scatterers of ashes on the waters
check the weather, then slip away
to lie on the beach.

But death, that scab, pays no attention
to the pickets and goes on
about his predatory business
with the conscience of a robber baron.

The strike continues for months
and corpses have to wait
in refrigerated warehouses
like supplicants in an unemployment line.
The old and young, diseased
and murdered, suicides and accidents,

so hungry for their little mouthful of earth
they don't even shiver, don't even notice
the cold. Until black spots of mourners
who can't finish their grief
begin to appear all over the city
like a rash on the streets.

Finally, the unburied dead outnumber
the newborn. Out of sheer critical mass,
the almost silent mutter of their souls
(like thousands of gray rubbing butterflies)
pollinates the air and defeats the season.
That spring, even the living
yearn only for ashes and dust.

Fog

My first hundred years of death
I'd like to spend driving
down this same road through the hills.
The same kind of music on the radio—Pergolesi,
Vivaldi, Telemann, over and over—
never wanting to stop, just
driving in the fog until I manage
to forget everything.

Only after that, maybe, a town
on the coast, another coast, a
seacoast I don't know. Just
a spot of sun between the cliffs,
then the village, three or four bars,
some houses, a hotel. A place
with umbrellas outside for lunch.

That's strange. The bartender, with
a cigaret in his mouth, absently
washing the glasses. I think
he was my friend, my sworn ally
when I was ten. He has
that same belonging look.
And the waiter. Leaning

against the tree, Isn't he—
the old man—Ignatz. My
grandfather's drinking buddy?
And there at the corner table,
relaxing, reading her book, waiting for
someone. Is this where
she lives now? My love on
the first day I met her.

The Saints

glare down at us and scowl,
while the angels smile
knowing how little of paradise
is reserved for the holy. An island perhaps—
if heaven were earth—surrounded by
ocean to quarantine their bile.

ART BECK is a poet, essayist, and translator whose work has appeared in books and magazines since the early 1970s. Translations of Rainer Maria Rilke's poems were published in *Etudes: A Rilke Recital* (Shanti Arts, 2020), which was a finalist for the 2021 Northern California Book Awards. His *Opera Omnia Or, a Duet for Sitar and Trombone, versions of the sixth-century CE North African Roman poet Luxorius* (Otis Books/Seismicity Editions, 2013) won the 2013 Northern California Book Award for translated poetry. *Mea Roma* (Shearsman Books, 2018), a 140-poem "meditative sampling" of Martial's epigram was awarded Honorable Mention in the American Literary Translators Association 2018 Cliff Becker Prize. In 2019, his poetic sequence *The Insistent Island* was published by Magra Books in its annual chapbook series. From 2009 through 2012, Beck was a regular contributor to *Rattle*, with essays on translating poetry under the rubric "The Impertinent Duet." His articles on the translator's art have appeared in *Jacket2, Your Impossible Voice, The Journal of Poetics Research, PN Review*, and *The Los Angeles Review of Books*. He makes his home in San Francisco.

PAUL VANGELISTI is the author of more than thirty books of poetry as well as being a noted translator from Italian. Recently, his sonnet sequence *Imperfect Music* was published in a limited, bilingual edition by Galleria Mazzoli Editore in Modena. In 2015 he edited for Grove Press, Amiri Baraka's posthumous collected poems, *S.O.S.: Poems, 1961–2014*. In 2006 Lucia Re's and his translation of Amelia Rosselli's *War Variations* won both the Premio Flaiano in Italy and the PEN-USA Award for Translation. In 2010 his translation of Adriano Spatola's *The Position of Things: Collected Poems, 1961–1992* won an Academy of American Poets Prize. He lives in Pasadena (California) and Bagnone (Italy).

SHANTI ARTS

NATURE • ART • SPIRIT

Please visit us online
to browse our entire book
catalog, including poetry
collections and fiction, books
on travel, nature, healing, art,
photography, and more.

Also take a look at our highly
regarded art and literary journal,
Still Point Arts Quarterly, which
may be downloaded for free.

WWW.SHANTIARTS.COM

www.ingramcontent.com/pod-product-compliance
Lightning Source LLC
Chambersburg PA
CBHW022013090426
42741CB00007B/1008